ROCK STAR CHIC

THE DARK SIDE OF HIGH FASHION

Curated by PATRICE FARAMEH Designed by SUSANNE SCHAAL

THE CURATED
COLLECTION™

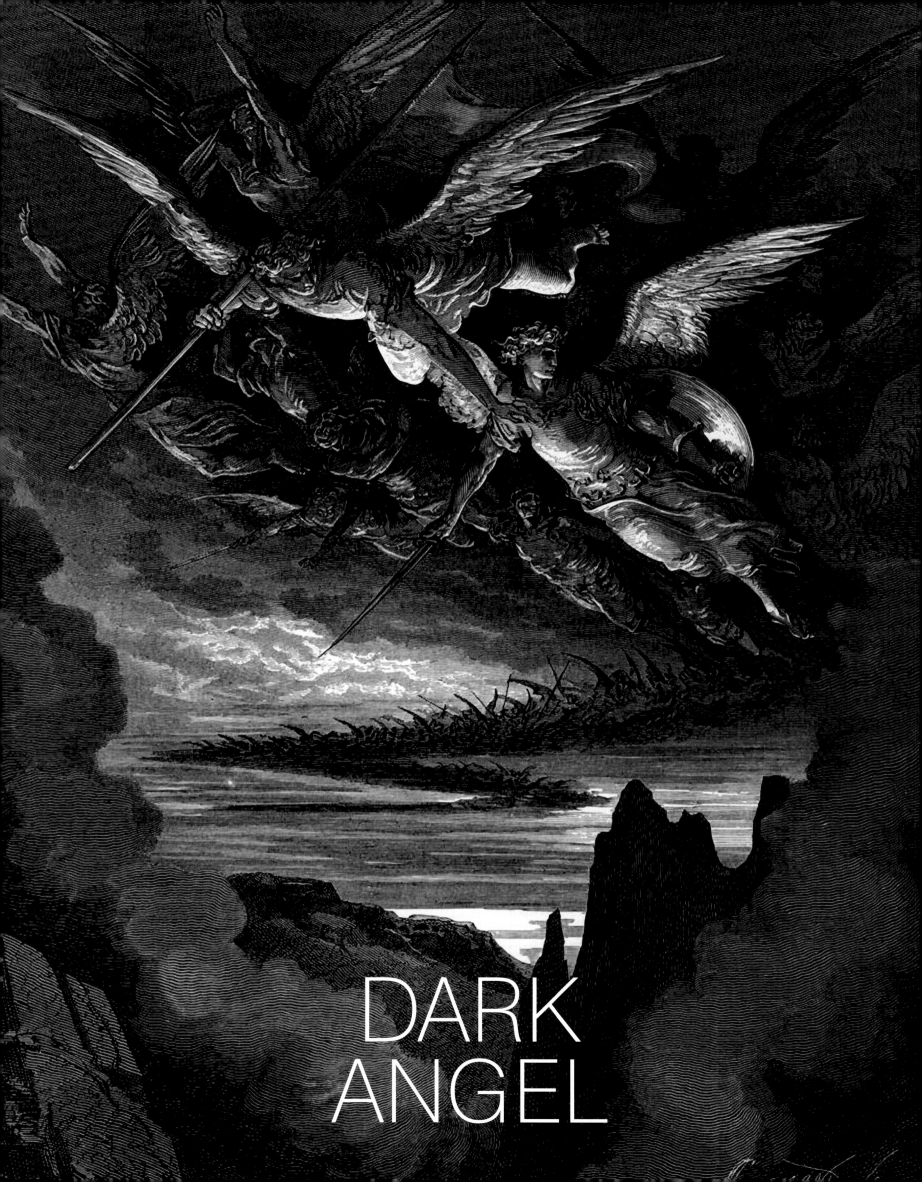

DARK
ANGEL

THE DARK ANGEL SACRIFICES BODY AND SPIRIT TO A MYSTERIOUS COVENANT. ELUDING THE INFLUENCES OF TRENDY EVANGELISTS, IT FOLLOWS A DEITY OF ITS OWN CREATION. The dark angel is brave enough to be vulnerable; when contained and restricted, it more readily contemplates the darkness within and without. A will as unbending as cast-iron drives its devotion. She partakes in austerities, covers her face in lace veils, binds herself in leather and strict silhouettes. His sartorial choices strengthen his resolve and passion, for he cannot remain anesthetized when he feels his body is bound. Cynical inquisition surrounds her. Free of defensive claims he makes no answer. Forsaking conventional modes of behavior, she favors extremes of stoicism, humility, and severity. Enduring these rituals, his purity remains intact and unsullied-a fortified inner sanctum amid a ruined city. They are not alone. She brushes past a figure in a dark hood just long enough to be penetrated by his eyes, as deep and fixed as hers. Resisting serpentine temptation, dark angels taste the rarest fruit.

PHOTOGRAPHER Yangshik Kong DESIGNER Golden Chix "Sweet as Poison"

PHOTOGRAPHER Barry Hollywood STYLIST James Rosenthal MODEL Jessica Pitti FASHION Top by Alon Livné; Pants by Dominic Louis; Belt by Zana Bayne

PHOTOGRAPHER Barry Hollywood STYLIST James Rosenthal MODEL Jessica Pitti
FASHION Leather Leotard by Bess; Necklace by Eddie Borgo; Hat by Zana Bayne; Shoes by Brian Atwood

PHOTOGRAPHER Barry Hollywood STYLIST James Rosenthal MODEL Jessica Pitti
FASHION Blazer and Leggings by Alon Livné; Rings by Eddie Borgo; Choker by Zana Bayne

PHOTOGRAPHER Yangshik Kong DESIGNER Golden Chix "Sweet as Poison"

PHOTOGRAPHER Khoa Bui DESIGNER Jessica L. Huang MODEL Katelyn Pascavis; Hair by Ashley Lynn Hall; Makeup by Nathan Hejl
ARTIST Gustave Doré ILLUSTRATION Gorgons and Hydras and Chimeras dire, from Book II of *Paradise Lost* by John Milton © Gustave Doré/Bridgeman Art Library

TOP: PHOTOGRAPHER Marc Lagrange "A Thousand Rings" BOTTOM: PHOTOGRAPHER Marc Lagrange "Millionaire"

16

PHOTOGRAPHER Marc Lagrange "Bonne"

PHOTOGRAPHERSCULPTOR Aoi Kotsuhiroi "Wet Moon, Hand Object"

Made with silk thread, human hair, pit-fired porcelain, phantom crystals, gold antique roman beads, bone, horn and urushi lacquer.

18

PHOTOGRAPHER/SCULPTOR Aoi Kotsuhiroi "Vertebra, Wrist Object"
Made with horn, bison leather, horsehair, urushi lacquer and gold antique roman beads.

PHOTOGRAPHER/SCULPTOR Aoi Kotsuhiroi "Dawn Ritual, Feet Object." Made with horns (heels), cherry tree wood, urushi lacquer and leather.

20

PHOTOGRAPHERSCULPTOR Aoi Kotsuhiroi "Scar of Memories, Feet Object" Made with horns (heels), cherry tree wood, urushi lacquer and leather.

DESIGNER Solange Azagury-Partridge "Ball Crusher Ring" Made with 18-karat white gold, pearl and enamel nails.

NEXT PAGE: PHOTOGRAPHER GL Wood STYLIST Michael Tucker MODEL Elana Santamatilde; Hair by Jennifer Yepez; Makeup by Vincent Oquendo

BODY ARTIST Jenai Chin ACCESSORIES Nails by Cassandra Lamar

PHOTOGRAPHER Daniel Jackson

PHOTOGRAPHER Callum Aldrin Smith STYLIST Daniel Boey DESIGNER BODYBOUND MODEL Philip Huang

NEXT PAGE: PHOTOGRAPHER DESIGNER Máximo Riera "Octopus Chair" Similarly to how man and nature depend on each other

PHOTOGRAPHER SCULPTOR Aoi Kotsuhiroi "Daydream, Neck Object"

Made with pit-fired porcelain skulls, human hair, silk thread, Japanese antique indigo fabric and antique black glass roman beads.

PHOTOGRAPHERS Ari Soffer and Shane Russeck DESIGNER Ari Soffer "Don't Fuck Around Cardinal Ring"

Made with pavé black diamonds with black diamond eyes. Many rock stars, including Axl Rose, have this ring in their personal collection.

PHOTOGRAPHER Terence Bogue DESIGNER Julia deVille "Claw Ring" Made with white gold, black rhodium and diamond.

PHOTOGRAPHER Kimberley Camilleri DESIGNER Sofia Fitzpatrick MODEL Meluxine

"Love Me In Your Head" "The Bruto" "The Sun Burst" "The Together Forever" "The Chatterbox" "The Hare Today Gone Tomorrow" skull rings (left to right).

PHOTOGRAPHER Erez Sabag **DESIGNER** Dror Benshitrit "Tron Chair"
Constructed out of roto-molded plastic with various shades of black and textural surfaces,
Tron Chair pays homage to the digital "Outlands" terrain in Tron.

PHOTOGRAPHER Nadir DESIGNER La Perla "Black Label collection FW 2007" Cage bustier made with whalebones, covered in satin and modeled by hand.

PHOTOGRAPHER Nadir DESIGNER La Perla "Black Label collection FW 2007" Transparent black bodysuit in which the lightness of the lace is overshadowed by lace inserts.

PHOTOGRAPHER Jarek Kotomski DESIGNER Fleet Ilya

PHOTOGRAPHER Luke Nugent DESIGNER Shinsuke Mitsuoka "BO(R)NE"

44

PREVIOUS PAGE: ARTIST Gustave Doré ILLUSTRATION Gorgons and Hydras and Chimeras dire, from
Book II of *Paradise Lost* by John Milton © Gustave Doré/Bridgeman Art Library
PHOTOGRAPHER/DESIGNER Stephen Webster "Lust" Made with 18-karat white gold with white diamonds
and a tanzanite central stone. Part of the "Seven Deadly Sins" collection.

VAMP
GLAM

ITS LURES ARE SET AND THE TERRITORY HAS BEEN STALKED. THE VAMPIRE GOTH IS READY TO HARVEST ITS PREY. Upon first glance it may look as demure as a doe or as prone as a kitten in the wilderness. Do not be fooled. This self-possessed creature is unrelenting in its mercuriality. It extends its bladelike claws, unleashes its chains, spreads its wings, and ruffles its slick, obsidian fur. Therianthropic, it will embody any number of forms. One thing remains the same its fearless sexuality takes on mythic proportions. Fierce and predatory when hunting after its desires, it is powerful, seductive, and unapologetic. It is in its nature to shift and transform; it is its biological destiny to bare its fangs and unfurl its taloned feet. Its sanguine instinct, sharp as a steel stiletto, never leads it astray.

PHOTOGRAPHER Billy Kidd DESIGNER Bliss Lau

PHOTOGRAPHER Chadwick Bell DESIGNER Cushnie et Ochs fall/winter 2010-2011

PHOTOGRAPHER Gábor Márton DESIGNER Dora Mojzes MODEL Nóra Anna Matisz; Hair by Tamas Tuzes; Makeup by Richard Fazekas ARTIST Gustave Doré ILLUSTRATION Satan rousing his troop of fallen angels, from Book 1 of *Paradise Lost* by John Milton © Gustave Doré/Bridgeman Art Library

PHOTOGRAPHER David Alexandre DESIGNER Rachel Freire

PHOTOGRAPHER Khoa Bui DESIGNER Jessica L. Huang STYLIST Rafael Linares
MODEL Lucy McIntosh; Hair by Whitney Willison; Makeup by Dana Delaney

PHOTOGRAPHER Mark Buenaobra **DESIGNER** Kermit Tesoro "Oil Spiller"

Most of designer Kermit Tesoro's shoes are paired with a clothing piece(s) but this shoe in particular was an isolated case. Oil Spiller combines beauty with toxicity, reinforcing the idea we try to prevent our lives from being messy or getting messed up by accidents and dangers, despite the fact that these mishaps create a good story.

PHOTOGRAPHER Ben Riggott DESIGNER Lascivious MODEL Jen Dawson; Hair by Koji Ichikawa; Makeup by Ken Nakano ACCESSORIES Atsuko Kudo

PHOTOGRAPHER Esad Cicic STYLIST Chantal Ritter MODEL Kat Cords ACCESSORIES Bangle by Regis Ales

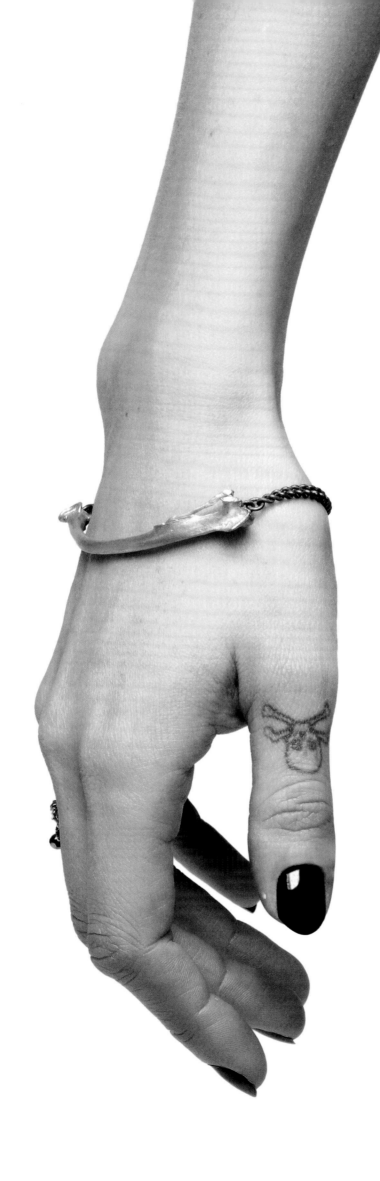

PHOTOGRAPHER Terence Bogue DESIGNER Julia deVille "Bone Bracelet Large" Made with sterling silver and enamel paint.
NEXT PAGE: PHOTOGRAPHER Adam Laycock DESIGNER Holly Hannah "Black Grasshopper Marquet"

PHOTOGRAPHER GL Wood STYLIST Michael Tucker MODEL Michaela Dietrich; Hair and Makeup by Ronnie Peterson FASHION Coat and Skirt by Christian Siriano; Top by Lie Sang Bong

FASHION Hervé Léger dress by Max Azaria; Coat by Costume National

PHOTOGRAPHER David Sessions DESIGNER Eleanor Amoroso

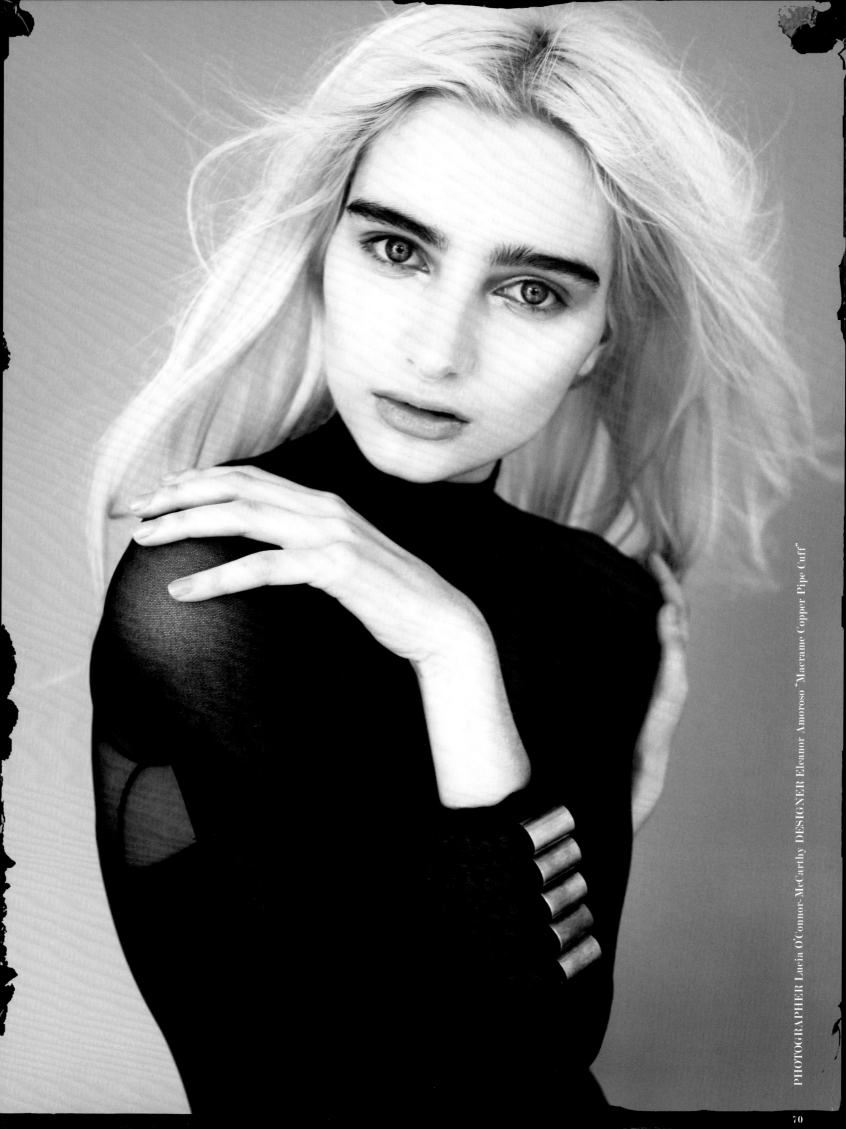

PHOTOGRAPHER Lucia O'Connor-McCarthy DESIGNER Eleanor Amoroso "Macrame Copper Pipe Cuff"

PHOTOGRAPHER DESIGNER Gisèle Ganne "Witching Hours Leather Collar"

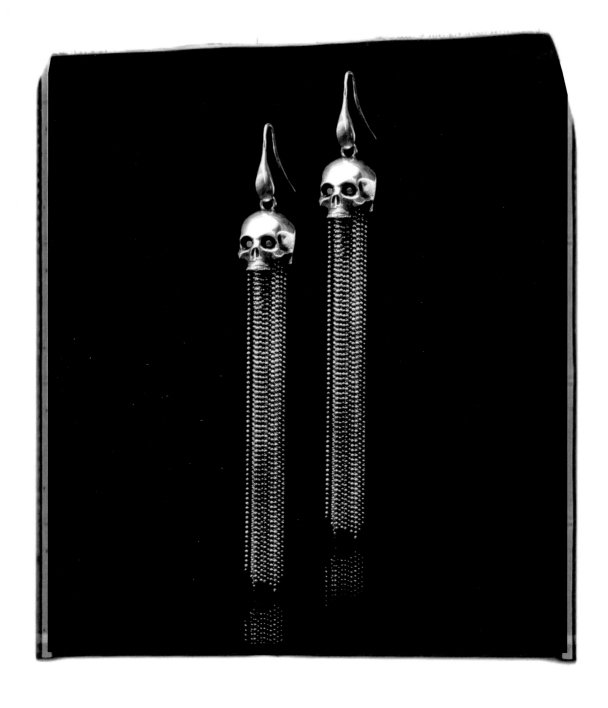

PHOTOGRAPHER Barry Hollywood STYLIST James Rosenthal MODEL Jessica Pitti FASHION (TOP) Leather Leotard by Bess; Coat by Nadia Tarr; Choker Necklace by Eddie Borgo; Hat by Zana Bayne; (BOTTOM) Leggings by Alon Livné; Shoes by Brian Atwood; (NEXT PAGE) Harness by Zana Bayne; Dress by Sally LaPointe; Shoes by Brian Atwood

PHOTOGRAPHER Oliver Kniest DESIGNER Kunza Corsetorium "S P E L L bound" leather restraint girdle

PHOTOGRAPHER/DESIGNER Theo Fennell; Made with 18-karat white gold, pavé diamonds (skull) and black diamonds (snake).

PHOTOGRAPHER Colin R. Singer MODEL Rick Genest

PHOTOGRAPHER Khoa Bui DESIGNER Jessica L. Huang

MODEL Katelyn Pascavis; Hair by Ashley Lynn Hall; Makeup by Nathan Hejl

DESIGNER Rad Hourani "Unisex Haute Couture collection #10"

ARTIST Gustave Doré ILLUSTRATION Satan flies toward the coast of Earth beneath, from Book III of *Paradise Lost* by John Milton

© Gustave Doré/Bridgeman Art Library

PHOTOGRAPHER Ralph Wenig (*Artsphere*) STYLIST Sheyma Gherabli PHOTOGRAPHER ASSISTANT Franck Aubert ((Courtesy of OOB Magazine)

MODEL Alex Yuryeva (*Silent*); Hair by Muriel Vancauwen, Makeup by Jabe (*B Agency*) FASHION Necklace by Odette Bombardier; Top by Jitrois

PHOTOGRAPHER Dewi Magz DESIGNER Tex Saverio "The Revelation"

ARTIST Gustave Doré ILLUSTRATION Satan in Council, from Book I of *Paradise Lost* by John Milton © Gustave Doré/Bridgeman Art Library

PHOTOGRAPHER Ssam Kim DESIGNER Golden Chix "Taxidermist's Tweezers"

PHOTOGRAPHER Hugh O'Malley DESIGNER BODYBOUND STYLIST Samuel Joseph Smith

PHOTOGRAPHER Gábor Márton DESIGNER Dora Mojzes
MODEL Nóra Anna Matisz; Hair by Tamas Tuzes; Makeup by Richard Fazekas

PREVIOUS PAGE: ARTIST Gustave Doré ILLUSTRATION Satan flies toward the coast of Earth beneath, from Book III of *Paradise Lost* by John Milton © Gustave Doré/Bridgeman Art Library

PHOTOGRAPHER/DESIGNER Stephen Webster "Jewels Verne Shark Bracelet" Set in 18-karat gold with silver and white diamonds, the *Jewels Verne Shark Bracelet* was inspired by the French author

Jules Verne's adventure novel *20,000 Leagues Under the Sea*.

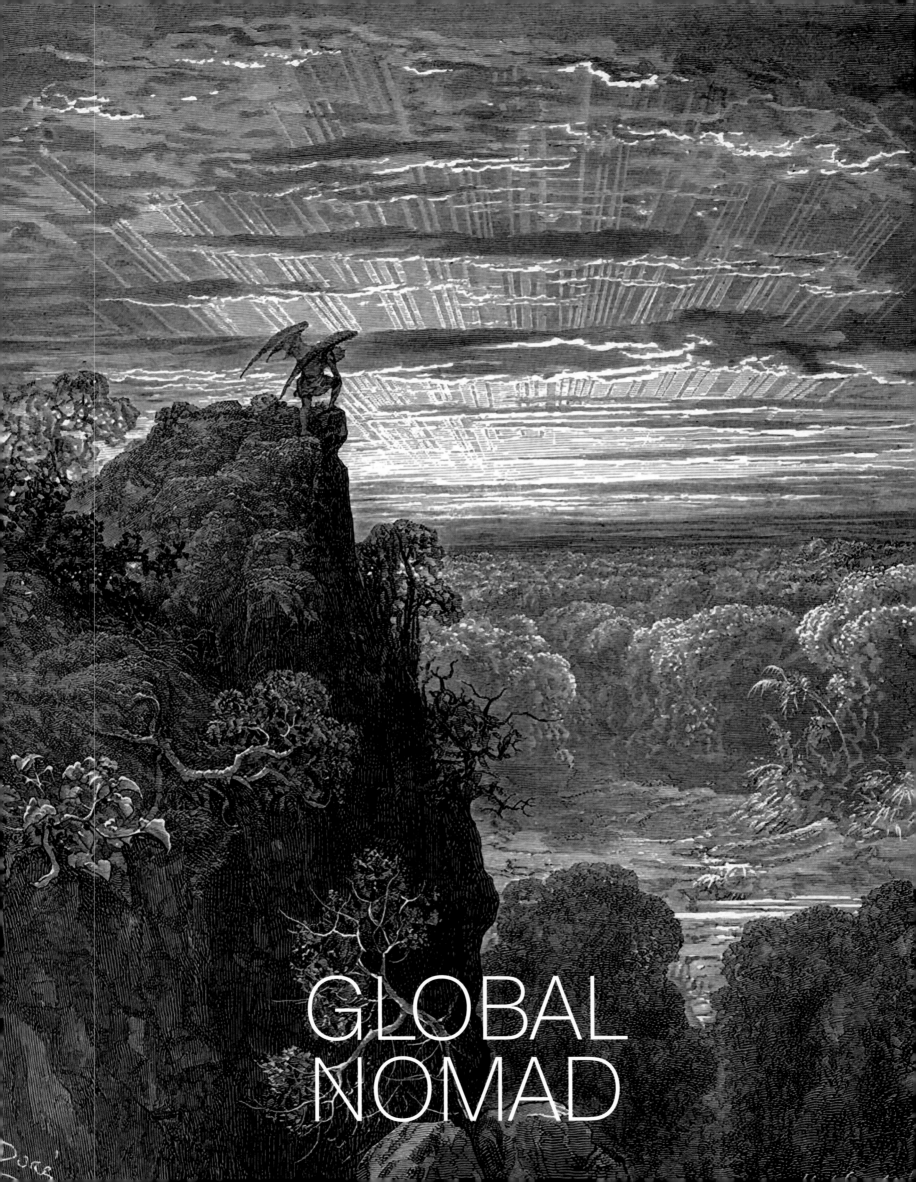

GLOBAL
NOMAD

THE GLOBAL NOMAD SEARCHES FOR SIGNS IN WHIRLING WINDS. DRAWN TO WHISPERS OF ANCIENT TALISMANS THAT LAY BURIED UNDER HOOVE-TRODDEN SOIL, THEY SEEK REMOTE LANDS UNTOUCHED BY THE FOLLY OF MAN. High up in the mountains, dark caverns hold forgotten secrets, while under the glowing embers of an orange and pink mesa sunset, the migratory patterns of buffaloes provide lost knowledge of the first man. They will adopt the guise of a spirit animal or jump on the back of a galloping horse to guide them wherever they may. Sturdy snakeskin boots carry them across long stretches of open road. Travel sways them like music, another outlet for their energy, another mode for self-expression. For the global nomad, clarity is found in the pulsating rhythm of the djembe and in the mystical riffs of a perpetually touring rock and roll band. Whether chasing the horizon, diving into the depths of an inky abyss, or shaking a tamborine to the point of transcendence, they search for freedom and the means by which to attain it.

PHOTOGRAPHER Fabrizio Rainone FASHION CONSULTANT Julia Clancey

MODEL Caroline Rausch; Hair by Sherman Hawthorne; Makeup by Andrea

FASHION Boots by Gina; Pendants and Rings by Stephen Webster; Swarovski nipplettes by Julia Clancey; Coat by Pam Hogg; Tights by Pamela Mann; Briefs by Myla

PHOTOGRAPHER Samantha West DESIGNER Bess NYC

PHOTOGRAPHER Samantha West DESIGNER Bess NYC

99

PHOTOGRAPHER Fabrizio Rainone FASHION CONSULTANT Julia Clancey
MODEL Caroline Rausch; Hair by Sherman Hawthorne; Makeup by Andrea
FASHION Waistcoat by Reem; Body Drape by Julia Clancey; Tights by Pamela Mann
ACCESSORIES Cuff by Julia Clancey; Bracelet and Rings by Stephen Webster; Shoes by Gina

PHOTOGRAPHER Rennio Maifredi DESIGNER Lost Art by Jordan Betten MODEL Elise Crombez

PHOTOGRAPHER Rennio Maifredi DESIGNER Lost Art by Jordan Betten MODEL Elise Crombez

PHOTOGRAPHER Jan Welters

PHOTOGRAPHER Pierre-Yves Toledano DESIGNER Springstoux

PHOTOGRAPHER Billy Kidd DESIGNER Bliss Lau

PHOTOGRAPHER Matthias Vriens-McGrath

PHOTOGRAPHER Kat + Duck Photography DESIGNER Castro MODEL Diandre Forrest

PHOTOGRAPHER Kat + Duck Photography DESIGNER Castro MODEL Diandre Forrest

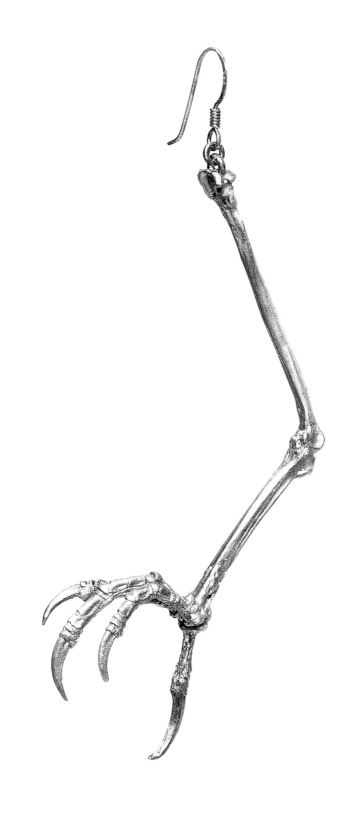

PHOTOGRAPHER Jeff P. Elstone II STYLIST James Rosenthal "Freyja" Inspired by the Norse goddess.

PHOTOGRAPHER Jeff P. Elstone II "L'Eclisse"

PHOTOGRAPHER Shane Russeck DESIGNER Ari Soffer MODEL Eve Mauro
"Nickerson Bourne Leather Bracelet" "Nickerson Bourne Buckle" "Long Horn Ring"

PHOTOGRAPHER Pierre-Yves Toledano DESIGNER Springsioux

NEXT PAGE: PHOTOGRAPHER Cheryl Rixon Davis DESIGNER Royal Order "Winged Skull Boots"

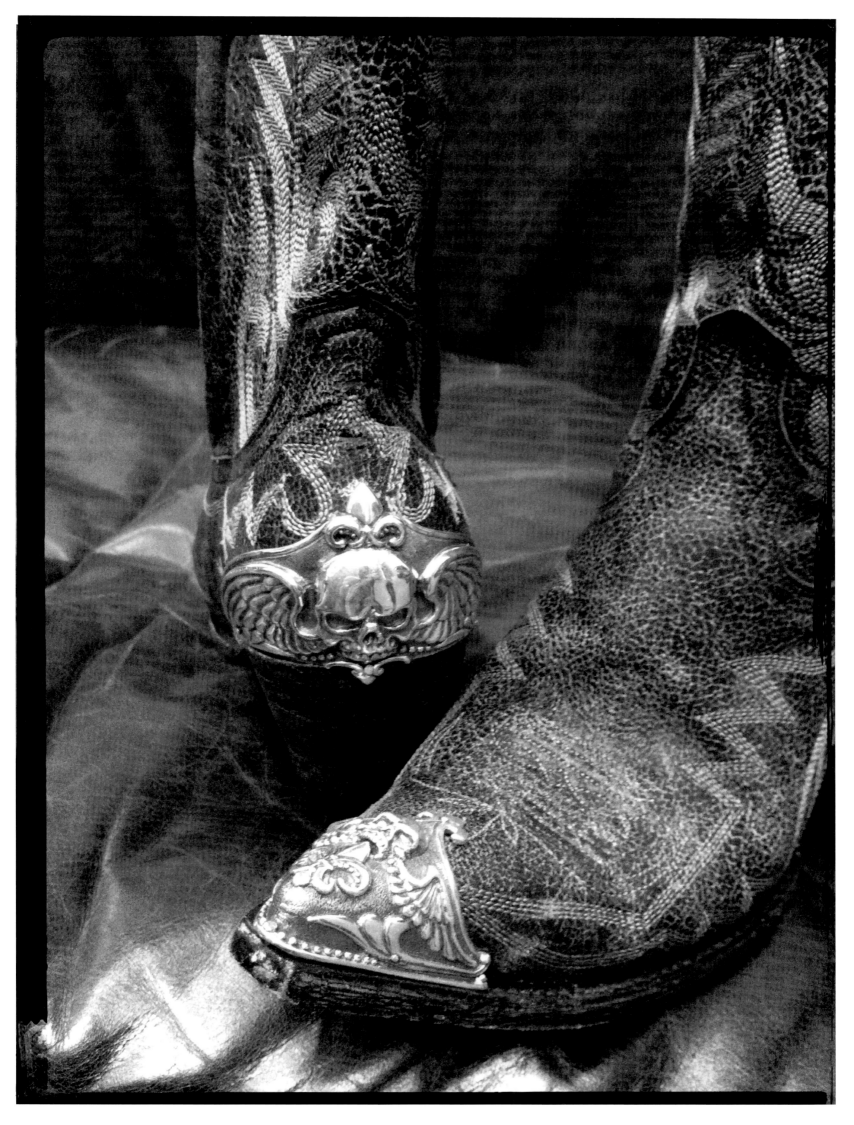

PHOTOGRAPHER Fabrizio Rainone FASHION CONSULTANT Julia Clancey
MODEL Caroline Rausch; Hair by Sherman Hawthorne; Makeup by Andrea
FASHION Catsuit by Pam Hogg; Shoes and Hat by Rab Goodwin ACCESSORIES Necklace and Cuff by John Yate

PHOTOGRAPHER Adrian Gaut **DESIGNER** Lost Art by Jordan Betten and McGuire Furniture
Made with King Cobra snakeskin, silver rings and leather fringe.

PHOTOGRAPHER Daniel Gabbay

DESIGNER Edra "Leather Works"

Leather Works Armchairs consist of approximately 400 pieces of hand-assembled, multi-textured leather.

PHOTOGRAPHER LutQman DESIGNER Lost Art by Jordan Betten
Made with alligator and leather.

PHOTOGRAPHER Caitlin Cronenberg DESIGNER Lost Art by Jordan Betten MODEL Hailey Clauson

PHOTOGRAPHER Caitlin Cronenberg DESIGNER Lost Art by Jordan Betten MODEL Hailey Clauson

PHOTOGRAPHER Ralph Wenig (Artsphere) STYLIST June Nakamoto STYLIST ASSISTANT Naoko Soeya PHOTOGRAPHER ASSISTANTS Franck Aubert and Thomas Appert MODEL Marija Piskac (WM) CELEBRITY Yohann Huget (Agence Atypique); Hair and Makeup by Angélik Iffennecker (Marie-France Thavonekham) FASHION (HIM) Crystal Skull Necklace by Swarovski

PHOTOGRAPHER Ruy Sanchez Blanco DESIGNER Lost Art by Jordan Betten MODEL Sarah Lamb

NEXT PAGE: PHOTOGRAPHER Rennio Maifredi DESIGNER Lost Art by Jordan Betten

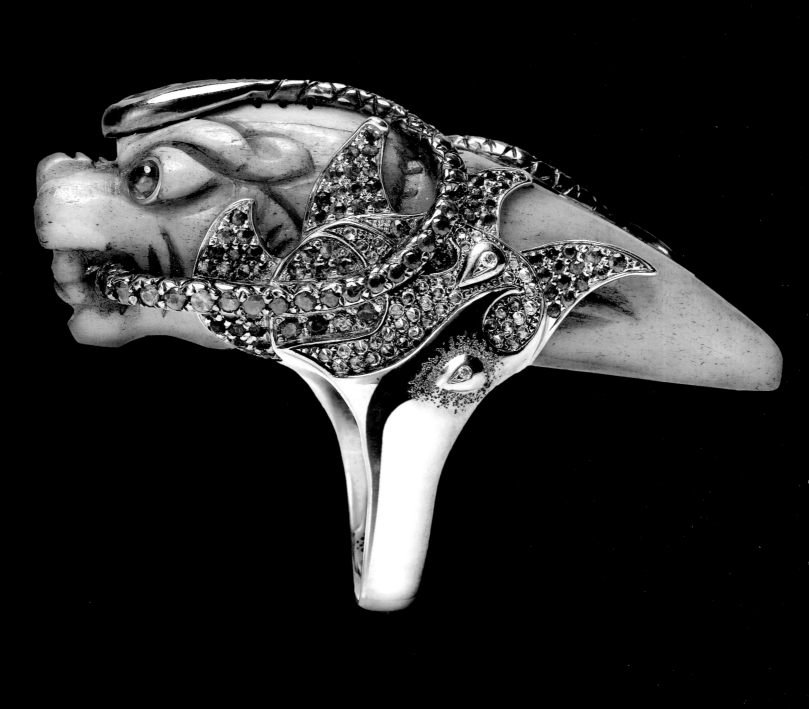

PHOTOGRAPHER Therese Aldgård DESIGNER Castro "Ying and Yang"

Inspired by the forces of nature fighting each other into the final evolution, a tiger. Made with antique tiger tooth bone, rubies, saphires, diamonds and 18-karat gold.

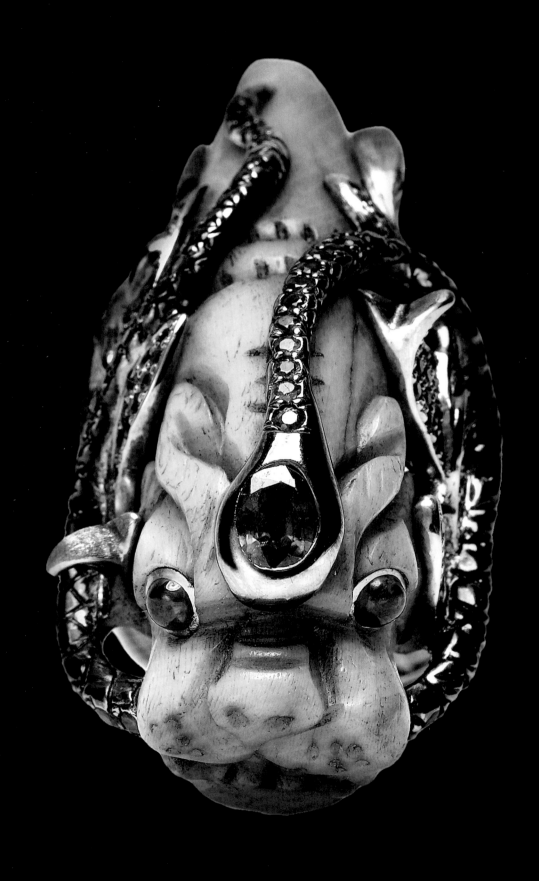

TOP: PHOTOGRAPHER Vlad Galat DESIGNER King Baby

BOTTOM: PHOTOGRAPHER Shane Russeck DESIGNER Ari Soffer "Perfect Collateral O.G. & N.C. Cross Bracelet" "Extra Large Don't Fuck Around Ring"

PHOTOGRAPHER Chek Wu MODEL Olivia Gordon

PHOTOGRAPHER Diego Indraccolo DESIGNER Rob Goodwin

PREVIOUS PAGE: ARTIST Gustave Doré ILLUSTRATION Adam and Eve plucking the fruits of the Garden
of Eden, from Book IV of *Paradise Lost* by John Milton © Gustave Doré/Bridgeman Art Library
PHOTOGRAPHER/DESIGNER Stephen Webster "The Temptation of Eve"
Made with 18-karat rose gold with black diamonds and rubies.

PHOTOGRAPHER Michel Dieuleks DESIGNER Paul Seville "The Spike Queen of Gallery 58" Developed and created through a passion for all things beautifully wrong, decadent and unreasonable.
NEXT PAGE: ARTIST Gustave Doré ILLUSTRATION Embryos and idiots, eremites and friars, white, black and gray with all their trumpery
from Book II of *Paradise Lost* by John Milton © Gustave Doré/Bridgeman Art Library

HARD
ROCK

THE HARDROCK FACTION HAS MADE THE CITY ITS PLAYGROUND. THEY STALK THE STREETS, A GRIMY ZONE WHERE SELF-ACTUALIZATION IS A HARD-WROUGHT STRUGGLE AGAINST ROUTINE CONFORMITY. They appropriate militaristic props, such as handcuffs, to reverse roles of authority. Brass knuckles and spikes complete their menacing wardrobe. The denizens of this urban landscape take on the hardy attributes of a species indigenous to the pavement. They don't shun spiders, rats or skulls, but embrace them as emblems of inherent mettle. With streetwise intelligence they navigate through the debris of the metropolis. Shrapnel, safety pins and studs inure them to the harsh environment, blackened by exhaust and smokestacks. Epidermis marked and metallized, they are individualized members of a gang whose manifesto is simple and poignant "Survive."

PHOTOGRAPHER Adam Laycock DESIGNER Holly Hannah "Pointer Nails"

PHOTOGRAPHER Esad Cicic STYLIST Chantal Ritter MODEL Jonas Wolfgang; Hair and Makeup by Richard Brockwell
FASHION Fur by Chantal Ritter; Jeans by Bess ACCESSORIES Necklace by WerkstattMünchen

153

PHOTOGRAPHER Esad Cicic STYLIST Chantal Ritter MODELS Jonas Wolfgang and Kat Cords; Hair and Makeup by Richard Brockwell

FASHION (HIM) Jeans by Bess ACCESSORIES Necklace by WerkstattMünchen

FASHION (HER) Beanie by RSVP; Blazer by Gucci vintage; Pants by Erro; Shoes by Alexander Wang

PHOTOGRAPHER Sarah McColgan DESIGNER Kerri Halpern of Madstone MAKEUP Victor Henao
"MadSpider" Double Finger Ring made with tsavorite, amethyst, and blue topaz set in 18-karat gold with .40 carat
white diamonds.

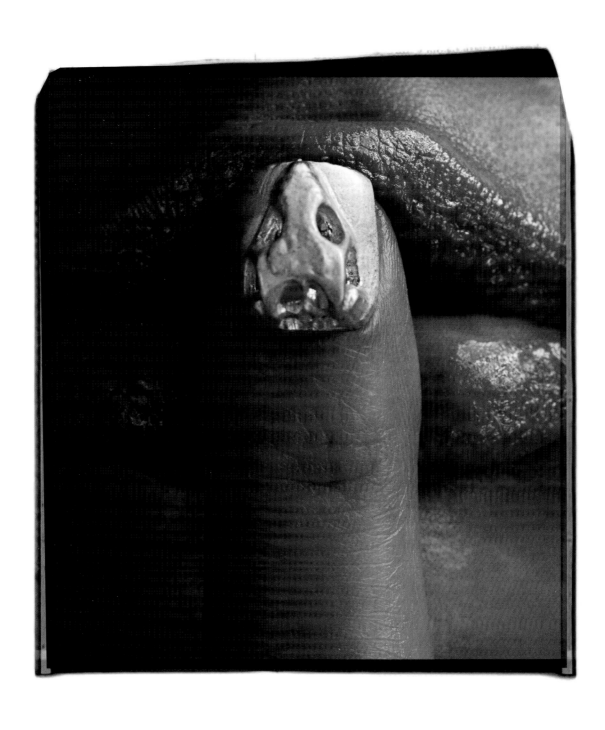

PHOTOGRAPHER Adam Laycock DESIGNER Holly Hannah "Silver Lizard Marguet"

PHOTOGRAPHERS Lydia Koch and Lauren Tennenbaum DESIGNER Lauren Tennenbaum

"Pomposity, Crystal and Metal"

Made with crystal and metal jewelry, and inspired by grandiose military costumes and the jewels of royalty.

158

PREVIOUS PAGE: PHOTOGRAPHER The Glint DESIGNER Úna Burke "RE.TREAT #8" Made with undyed vegetable-tanned leather
and solid brass fittings. ARTIST Gustave Doré ILLUSTRATION Satan Rousing His Troop Of Fallen Angels, from Book I of *Paradise Lost*
© Gustave Doré/Bridgeman Art Library
PHOTOGRAPHER The Glint DESIGNER Úna Burke

PHOTOGRAPHERS Alfredo Albertone and Monica Feudi DESIGNER Prada

PHOTOGRAPHER Marco Bertani DESIGNER Dsquared²

PHOTOGRAPHERS Ari Soffer and Shane Russeck DESIGNER Ari Soffer "Don't Fuck Around Knuckles"
Limited edition piece, made with diamonds and rubies.

PHOTOGRAPHER Tommy Ton

PHOTOGRAPHER Mark Buenaobra DESIGNER Kermit Tesoro

PHOTOGRAPHER John-Paul Pietrus DESIGNER Bordelle "Bondage Angelo dress - Bordelle exclusive"

PREVIOUS PAGE: PHOTOGRAPHER Jeffrey Menolte DESIGNER Jessica L. Huang MODEL Emma Balsyte; Hair by Danielle Huacuja; Makeup by Pa Kou Xion

PHOTOGRAPHER The Glint DESIGNER Úna Burke

Made with handcrafted vegetable-tanned leather and brass spike fittings.

PHOTOGRAPHER Kimberley Camilleri JEWELRY Sofia Fitzpatrick MODEL Meluxine
"Thunderbolt" "The Love Me I'm In Your Head" "The Brutto" "The Sun Burst" skull rings (left to right).

174

PHOTOGRAPHER Hugh O'Malley DESIGNER BODYBOUND STYLIST Samuel Joseph Smith MODEL Philip Huang

PHOTOGRAPHER Adam Laycock DESIGNER Holly Hannah "Single Thorn Marguet"
NEXT PAGE: PHOTOGRAPHER Horacio Salinas

PHOTOGRAPHER GL Wood STYLIST Angella N. MODEL Marilia Ferreira; Makeup by Cynthia Rose
FASHION Cropped moto jacket by Sally LaPointe; Leather detailed leggings by Lina Osterman; Stockings by Emilio Cavallini; Socks by Wigwam; Shoes by Bess

PHOTOGRAPHER GL Wood STYLIST Angella N. MODEL Marilia Ferreira; Makeup by Cynthia Rose
FASHION Spiked bikini top by Dain Kalas Archive; Leather pants with silver detail by Sally LaPointe

PHOTOGRAPHER Esad Cicic STYLIST Chantal Ritter SHOES Jeffery Campbell

TOP: PHOTOGRAPHER Fabrizio Rainone FASHION CONSULTANT Julia Clancey MODEL Caroline Rausch
ACCESSORIES Bracelet and Ring by Stephen Webster; Necklace by Loba Vete
BOTTOM: PHOTOGRAPHER Viktor Vauthier DESIGNER Chau Har Lee "Steel Heels" Made with stainless steel and leather.

182

PHOTOGRAPHER Fabrizio Raimone FASHION CONSULTANT Julia Clancey MODEL Caroline Rausch
FASHION Tights by Henry Holland; Necklace by Julia Clancey; Shoes by Rob Goodwin; Ring by Stephen Webster

DESIGNER Francesco Scognamiglio "Metal Corset" fall/winter 2009/2010

ARTIST Gustave Doré **ILLUSTRATION** Satan rousing his troop of fallen angels, from Book I of *Paradise Lost* by John Milton

© Gustave Doré/Bridgeman Art Library

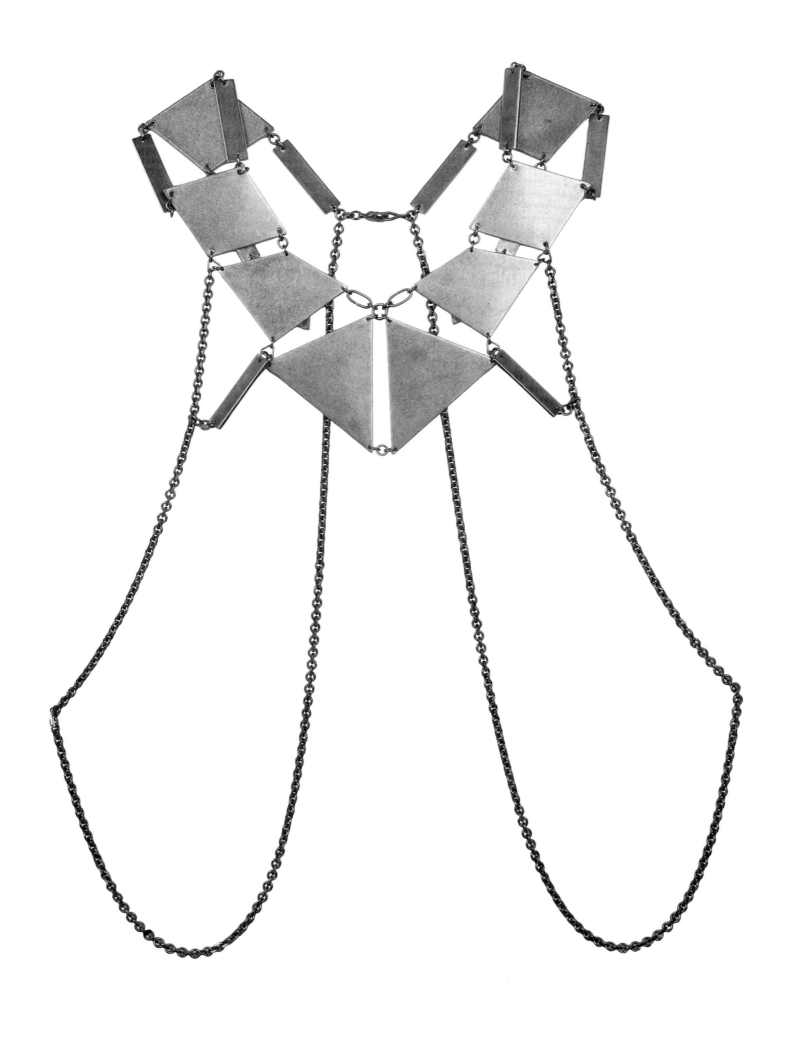

PHOTOGRAPHER Jarrod Turner DESIGNER Bliss Lau

2292-3

186

PHOTOGRAPHER Lara Giliberto JEWELRY Betony Vernon "Second Skin Hand Piece #1" Made with sterling silver.

PHOTOGRAPHER Ralph Wenig (Artsphere) STYLIST Sheyma Gherabli PHOTOGRAPHER ASSISTANT Franck Aubert (Courtesy of OOB Magazine)
MODEL Alex Yuryeva (Silent); Hair by Muriel Vancauwen (B Agency); Makeup by Jabe (B Agency); Manicure by Kathy (B Agency)
FASHION Headpiece by Odette Bombardier; Ring by Swarovski

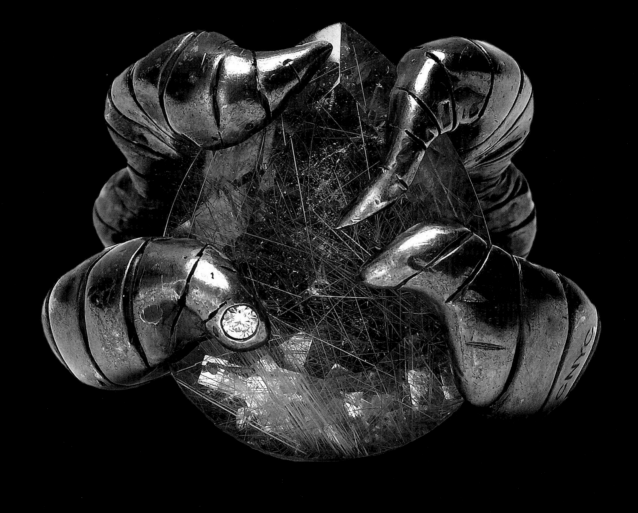

PHOTOGRAPHER Therese Aldgård DESIGNER Castro "Dinal"

Inspired by prehistoric stones and dinosaur tales. Made with sterling silver, rutilated quartz and white diamonds.

PHOTOGRAPHER Barry Hollywood STYLIST Danny Rosenthal FASHION Top by Jen Kao, Ear Cuff by LOMO MAKE-UP ARTIST Gustave Doré ILLUSTRATION Ithuriel and Zephon, from Book IV of *Paradise Lost* by John Milton © Gustave Doré Bridgeman Art Library

FUTURE
PUNK

IMAGINE A WORLD WHERE THERE ARE NO RULES.
THE LIMITS OF BEHAVIOR HAVE BEEN BLOWN AWAY,
REPLACED BY A DYSTOPIA THAT IS TERRIFYING IN
ITS PERFECTION. The imminent next step of rapid evolution has
taken place, technology has created an unprecedented breed of human.
It alone is adaptable to this strange new topogrophy, Philip K. Dick's
portentous literary vision come to life. The future punk crawls out of the
drek of the past in a lithe catsuit. She slices her way through the bonds
of tradition with icy, metallic weaponry. Finally, she reaches the apex.
A new planet has just begun orbit around earth; she unveils her exquisite
new skin under its prismatic glow.

PHOTOGRAPHER Kai Z Feng

PHOTOGRAPHER Kenneth Willardt STYLIST Sciascia Gambaccini MODEL Nik de Berry; Hair by Felix Fischer; Makeup by Regine Thorre

PHOTOGRAPHER GL Wood STYLIST Anna Katsanis MODEL Taylor Bagley; Hair by Nikki Nelms; Makeup by Roshar
FASHION Fur and Dress by Roberto Cavalli; Fishnet dress by Hervé Léger ACCESSORIES Earrings by Chanel

PHOTOGRAPHER Jungwon Park DESIGNER Yong Kyun Shin

PHOTOGRAPHER Jeffrey Menolte Jessica L. Huang DESIGNER Jeffrey Menolte MODEL Emma Balsyte; Hair by Danielle Huacuje; Makeup by Pa Kou Xiong

204

PHOTOGRAPHER Milana Bosnic DESIGNER Ivana Pilja "Semi Song collection"

PHOTOGRAPHER Barry Hollywood STYLIST James Rosenthal MODEL Jessica Pitti
FASHION Top by Valentina Kova; Pants by Daniel Silverstain ACCESSORIES Neckpiece by Daniel Silverstain; Finger claws by Mordikai; Shoes by Brian Atwood

206

PHOTOGRAPHER Barry Hollywood STYLIST James Rosenthal MODEL Jessica Pitti
FASHION Skeleton body harness by Zana Bayne; Motorcycle jacket by Bess

PHOTOGRAPHER Junichi Kikuchi DESIGNER BODYBOUND

NEXT PAGE: PHOTOGRAPHER Joanna Krause SHOE DESIGNER Netta Makkonen

PHOTOGRAPHER GL Wood STYLIST Anna Katsanis MODEL Taylor Bagley; Hair by Nikki Nelms; Makeup by Roshar

FASHION Leather studded jacket by Topshop; Zipper top by H&M; Miniskirt by D&G; Shoes by Fendi; Glasses by Ray Ban

DESIGNER Alexander McQueen "Armadillo Shoes" spring/summer 2010
NEXT PAGE: PHOTOGRAPHER Arron Dunworth DESIGNER Arajo

PHOTOGRAPHER Milana Bosnic DESIGNER Ivana Pilja "Semi Song collection"
NEXT PAGE: DESIGNER Yong Kyun Shin

PHOTOGRAPHER Balint Barna DESIGNER Dora Mojzes "Alien army" fall/winter 2012/2013 Inspired by the movie Prometheus.
STYLIST Igor Deseatnikov MODELS Kate Kondas (Nathalie models) and Monika Jabloczky (Visage models); Hair by Brigi Uheresik-Hairclub; Makeup by Natasa Kovalik

PHOTOGRAPHER Josh Olins

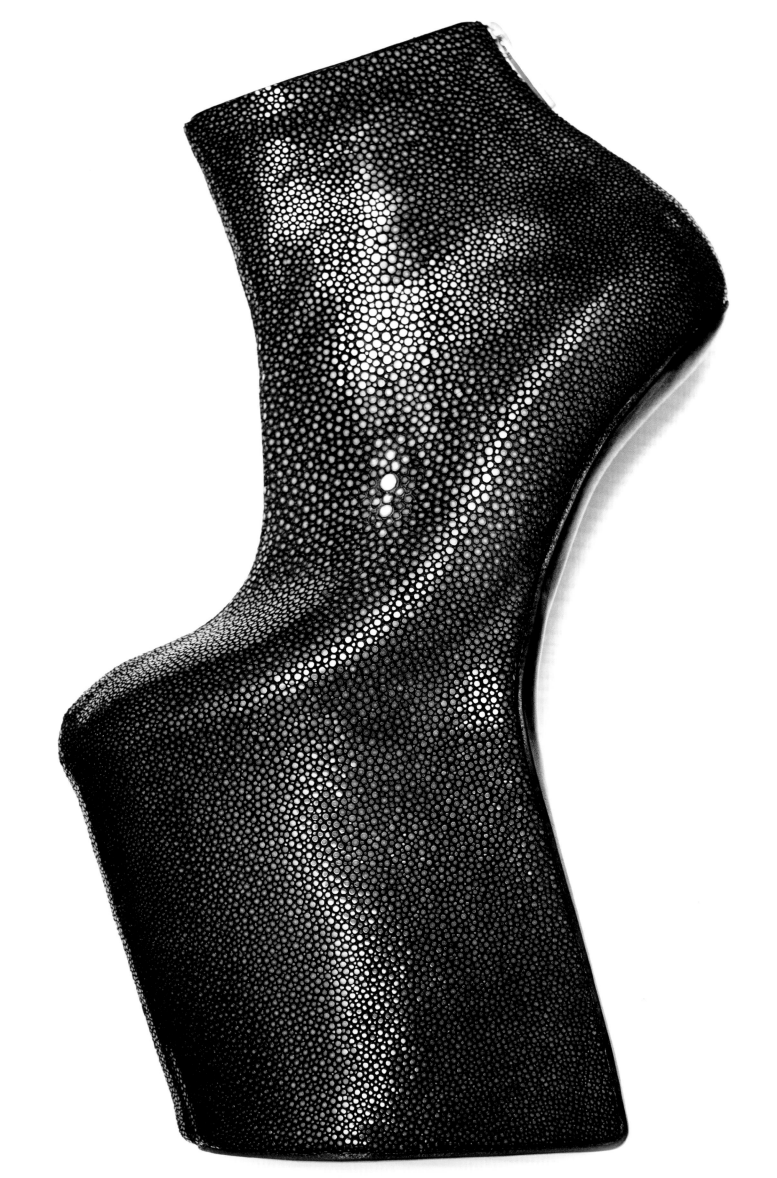

TOO FAST TO LIVE too young to die

PHOTOGRAPHER Esad Ćićić STYLIST Chantal Ritter MODEL Kat Cords; Hair and Makeup by Richard Brockwell

FASHION Beanie by RSVP; Blazer by Gucci vintage; Pants by Erro; Shoes by Alexander Wang

NEXT PAGE: PHOTOGRAPHER Esad Ćićić

My deepest gratitude to all of the highly creative designers, photographers, brands, and stylists who understand how to perfectly create the alluring, dangerous, and sultry side of high fashion. These creative spirits make it possible to love and live a beautifully dark existence.

Any omissions for copy or credit are unintentional, and appropriate credit will be given in future editions if such copyright holders contact the publisher.

All images have been supplied by courtesy of the respective designers, stylists, and photographers including all of the special instances below

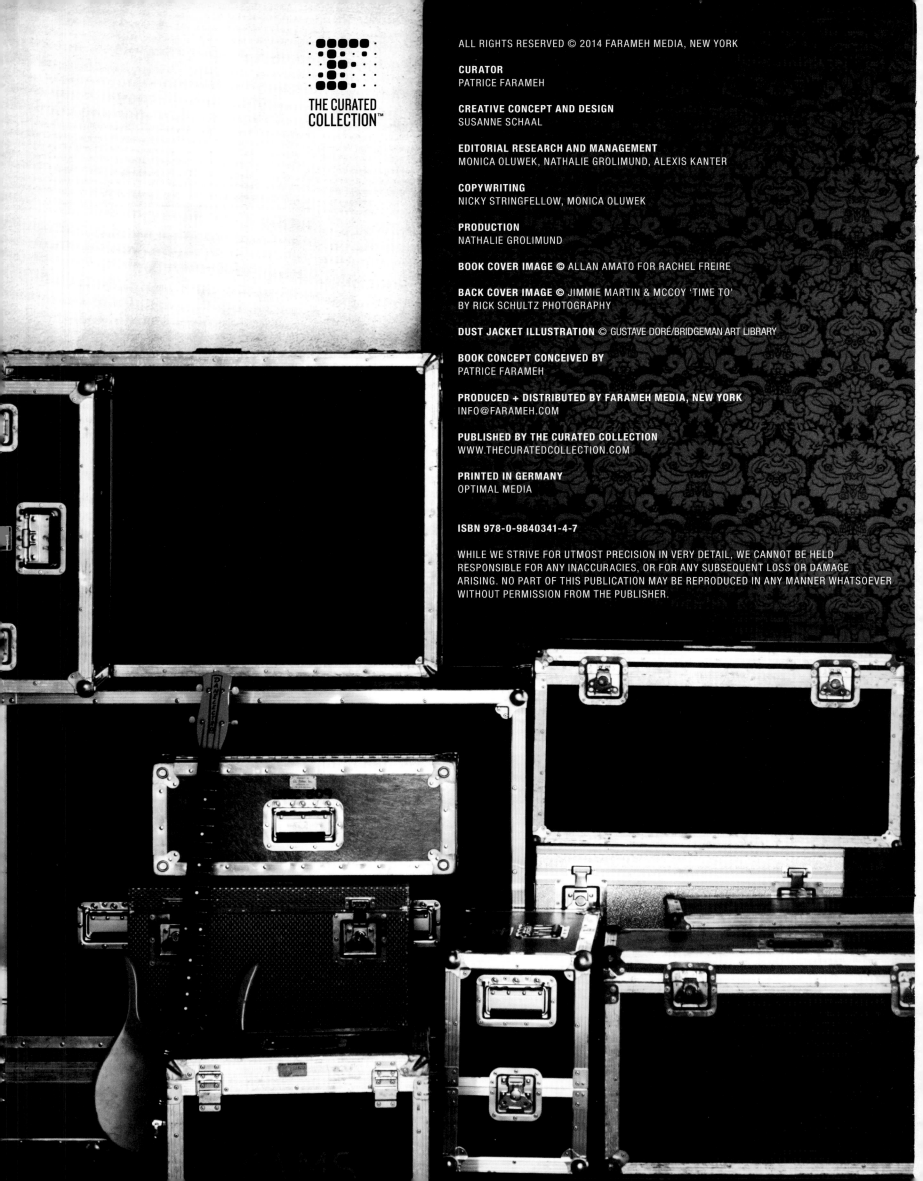

THE CURATED
COLLECTION™

CURATOR
PATRICE FARAMEH

CREATIVE CONCEPT AND DESIGN
SUSANNE SCHAAL

EDITORIAL RESEARCH AND MANAGEMENT
MONICA OLUWEK, NATHALIE GROLIMUND, ALEXIS KANTER

COPYWRITING
NICKY STRINGFELLOW, MONICA OLUWEK

PRODUCTION
NATHALIE GROLIMUND

BOOK COVER IMAGE © ALLAN AMATO FOR RACHEL FREIRE

BACK COVER IMAGE © JIMMIE MARTIN & MCCOY 'TIME TO'
BY RICK SCHULTZ PHOTOGRAPHY

DUST JACKET ILLUSTRATION © GUSTAVE DORÉ/BRIDGEMAN ART LIBRARY

BOOK CONCEPT CONCEIVED BY
PATRICE FARAMEH

PRODUCED + DISTRIBUTED BY FARAMEH MEDIA, NEW YORK
INFO@FARAMEH.COM

PUBLISHED BY THE CURATED COLLECTION
WWW.THECURATEDCOLLECTION.COM

PRINTED IN GERMANY
OPTIMAL MEDIA

ISBN 978-0-9840341-4-7